This richly illustrated booklet takes us, by means of a collection of traditional recipes, on a little journey around Alsace. It presents a variety of easy-to-prepare country dishes which have been handed down from generation to generation. These dishes were conditioned by the way to life of our forefathers, the produce of their lands, their hunting and their fishing. They have withstood the test of time firstly in families eager to preserve a gastronomic heritage and, secondly, on the menus of our restaurants and « Kachele » where people flock today to try to recapture the flavour of the dishes of days gone by.

The choice of recipes has been limited to family specialities, everyday fare, dishes which are simple to prepare and relatively unknown because, perhaps, they are not spectacular. They will serve a family of 5-6 people. That is why this little collection of recipes does not contain such recipes as « matelote » (a fish stew found mainly in coastal restaurants) for example, nor the sumptuous « foie gras de Strasbourg » which appears on the menus of the most expensive gastronomic restaurants.

We have tried to reset the cooking of Alsace in its rather intimate context, to give it its individuality by following traditional procedures and to trace the origin and history of certain dishes.

To conclude, we will quote Georges Spetz in « Alsace gourmande » who wrote in 1913 ---

« ... I, too, will become the apostle and patron
Of simple, natural and healthy cooking.
I shall not boast of rich sauces,
Complicated dishes or exciting stews ;
But the well-kept secrets of our old families
Handed down with love from mother to daughter,
The dishes and desserts on which I feasted
Sixty years ago when I was a child... ».

Potage aux pommes de terre
« Grumbeeresupp » or « Hardaepfelsupp »
Potato soup

750 g. potatoes / 1 leek / 1 large onion / 1 sprig parsley and chervil / small tub of thick cream / 50 g. butter / a little oil / 1 1/2 lit. stock or water / salt, pepper, nutmeg / croûtons fried in butter.

Peel and chop the onion and brown in a little oil. Slice the leeks and add. Season.

Peel and thinly slice the potatoes ; place on top of the onions and leeks. Simmer with a little stock (10 minutes). Add the remainder of the liquid, chopped parsley and chervil. Cook on medium heat for about 30 minutes. Puree the soup in a vegetable mill ; thicken with the cream or fresh milk, adjust seasoning, add a knob of butter and grated nutmeg. Serve piping hot with croûtons (fried in butter).

This soup can also be served over slices of Strasbourg sausages.

Potage à la bière
« Biersupp »
Beer soup

1 onion / 1 1/2 lit. chicken stock / 33 cl. light ale / 200 g. breadcrumbs / 30 g. butter / salt, pepper, grated nutmeg / small pot fresh cream / croûtons fried in butter.

Chop the onion and brown in the butter. Add the stock, then the beer, sprinkle over the breadcrumbs, season and cook for about 25 minutes. Pass the soup through a fine vegetable mill, and thicken with the cream. Add a pinch of nutmeg and serve with croûtons (optional).

Potage à l'oseille
« Surampfersupp » or « Grieni Supp »
Sorrel soup

1 large handful of sorrel leaves / parsley, chervil / 1 lit. stock / small tub cream / 75 g. butter / 50 g. flour / 2 egg yolks / salt, pepper / croûtons (optional).

Chop sorrel finely and lightly fry in butter. Add the flour and bring to the boil stirring constantly. Add warm stock and cook for about 5 minutes. Season, thicken with the 2 beaten egg yolks, cream, chopped parsley and chervil. Stir and serve hot with fried croûtons (optional).

Potage à la farine grillée
« Gebrenndi Mehlsupp »
Toasted flour soup

6 table spoons flour / small pat butter / 1 small tub cream / salt, pepper / croûtons / 1 1/2 lit. stock.

Pour the flour into a heavy pan and cook on a gentle heat stirring constantly with a wooden spoon until the flour turns golden brown. Add the stock and cook for 15 minutes being careful to avoid lumps forming. Before serving, season, add butter and cream. Pour into soup tureen and add croûtons fried in butter.

Potage aux lentilles à l'alsacienne
« Linsesupp »
Lentil soup à l'alsacienne

250 g. lentils / 1 leek / parsley / 2-3 carrots / 2 potatoes / 2 lit. water / 1 bay leaf / 2 cloves / 1 medium onion / 200 g. smoked bacon / 1 Strasbourg sausage per person / small tub cream or cup milk / salt, pepper.

Clean and wash the lentils and leave to soak for 2 hours or overnight. Cover with 2 lit. water. Season. Add the diced vegetables, chopped parsley, bacon, bay leaf and onion (spiked with the cloves). Cook over a low heat for 2 hours. A few minutes before serving add the Strasbourg sausages. Adjust the seasoning and add cream or milk. For a more nourishing soup thicken with a light roux sauce and pass through a vegetable mill.

Suggestion : similar soups can be made using a base of peas (Erbsesupp) or dried haricot beans (Bohnesupp).

Potage aux « Riwele »
« Riwelesupp »
Soup with « riwele » (dumplings)

125 g. flour / 2 eggs / 2 lit. good meat stock / salt, pepper, nutmeg / parsley or chervil.

Mix the flour, eggs and seasoning. Knead into a dough. Roll with the palm of the hand into long, thin « quenelles » (dumplings) - (« Riwele » cf. « riwe » = to rub). Poach the « Riwele » in the rich stock and sprinkle with chopped herbs.

Bouillon de bœuf aux quenelles de moelle
« Fleischsupp mit Marikknepfle »
Beef broth with marrow-bone quenelles

Broth :
1 kg. beef (top rib, silverside, blade, chęek) / some bones / 3 lit. cold water / carrots / turnip / leek / small green cabbage / stick celery / parsley / onion (spiked with 2 cloves) / bay leaf / 2 freshly grilled pea-pods / salt, pepper, nutmeg.

Place all the above ingredients in a cooking pot. Simmer for 3 hours. The 2 grilled pea-pods give the liquid its fine golden colour : skim and sieve the stock. Place meat and vegetables on one side.

Marrow-bone quenelles
150 g. marrow-bone jelly melted in a « bain-marie » / 2 eggs / 75 g. breadcrumbs / 1 table spoon flour / 1 table spoon semolina / finely chopped parsley, chervil / salt, pepper, nutmeg.

Mix all the ingredients and the marrow-bone jelly with a fork and form small balls about 1.5 cm in diameter (they swell during cooking). Poach in the stock for 10 minutes but do not boil. If the balls begin to break up add a little more flour.

The beef broth and marrow-bone quenelles should be served very hot and dusted with chopped herbs ; some vermicelli or small pieces of toast may be added.

In Alsace, pot-au-feu was the traditional Sunday meal. After the marrow-bone soup, the meat and vegetables reserved from the broth were served complemented by a hot or cold horse-radish sauce, accompanied by side-salads (raw or cooked grated carrot, cucumber, raw grated celery, cooked beetroot) as well as small roast potatoes.

Potage aux crêpes
« Schuebaendelsupp »
Soup with pancakes

2 lit. good beef stock / 3 medium pancakes / parsley, chervil / salt, pepper, nutmeg / small glass milk.

Cut the pancakes into thin strips (« lacets ») and poach for 10 minutes in the seasoned stock. Add milk and chopped herbs.

Beef broth with marrowbone dumplings. (Photo E.H. Cordier)

Sauce au raifort froide
« Kalter Merettich »
Cold horse-radish sauce

200 g. finely grated horse-radish / 200 g. breadcrumbs soaked in milk and drained / medium tub fresh cream / pinch sugar / 1 tsp. mustard / 1 table spoon vinegar.

Soak grated horse-radish in a little warm stock (10 minutes) until it swells. In a bowl, mix breadcrumbs, vinegar and mustard ; add horse-radish and mix well. Add cream, salt and sugar. Serve sauce cold.

Horse-radish sauce is a marvellous accompaniment for the meat and vegetables from a pot-au-feu, cold meats as well as certain roasts.

Since the Middle Ages raw grated horse-radish (with salt and vinegar) has been included in the range of salads and, according to one XVIth century doctor, was pronounced « an excellent hors-d'œuvre » ! At the beginning of winter the peasants used to buy their stock of mustard and horse-radish, to make sure they had enough to last them through the season.

Sauce vinaigrette
Vinaigrette dressing

1 hard boiled egg / 2 tbsp. vinegar / 4 tbsp. oil / 1 tsp. mustard / salt, pepper / chopped parsley and chives.

In a bowl make a sauce with the oil, vinegar, salt, pepper and mustard.

Beat with whisk to thicken.

On a plate finely mash the egg and add to dressing.

To be served immediately as the oil and vinegar will separate quickly.

Salade de pommes de terre
« Grumbeeresalad » or « Hardaepfelsalad »
Potato salad

1 kg. potatoes / 1 small onion / 1 glass wine winegar / parsley, chives / salt, pepper / 1 small tub cream / a little stock / a little mustard (optional).

Bake the potatoes in their jackets, cut into thin slices and dry carefully. In a bowl add the vinegar and stock to the finely chopped onions, salt, pepper, cream and mustard. Coat the potatoes with this mixture, sprinkle with chopped herbs and mix without breaking the slices of potato.

This potato salad accompanies Alsace charcuterie. It can be served warm with Knacks, black pudding or smoked pork shoulder.

Suggestions : Add small pieces of browned bacon (in this case use less salt).
Add a few chopped gherkins to the salad.

Salade de betteraves rouges
« Rotrahnesalad » or « Gullerilappelsalad »
Beetroot salad

About 10 beetroot / 1 glass vinegar / clove garlic / bay leaf / 2 cloves / medium onion / salt, pepper / 1 tbsp. oil / boiling salted water.

Trim beetroot and wash. Cook in salted water, peel and cut into thin slices. Marinade in a bowl in the vinegar, salt, pepper, finely chopped garlic and a little chopped onion for several days. Before serving adjust seasoning. Garnish with onion rings and sprinkle with a little oil. This salad is often served with the meat from a pot-au-feu.

Salade de pissenlits
Dandelion salad

500 g. dandelions / 150 g. piece of lean smoked bacon / salt, pepper, onion / a little vinegar.

Wash the dandelion leaves several times, drain and place in a salad bowl. Cut the bacon into cubes, brown in the oil and add to the salad. Place vinegar in the warm pan then pour over the salad.

Mixed salad « Cervila un Schwitzerkaessalaedel »

(Photo taken at the Winstub « Au Meiselocker » in Strasbourg by E.H. Cordier)

Asparagus and accompaniments.
(Photo A. Loviton)

Salade mixte
« Cervila un Schwitzerkaessalaedel »
Mixed salad

Saveloy salad :
6 saveloys / 1 onion or 3 shallots / salt, pepper, vinegar, oil / yolk of hard boiled egg / mustard to taste.

Peel saveloys, cut in half lengthways, cut incision in their bulbous part. Sprinkle with finely chopped parsley and onions. Coat with a vinaigrette dressing to which the yolk has been added.

The saveloy salad can be served as it is, on a bed of green salad surrounded by quarters of hard-boiled egg and slices of tomato.

Gruyère salad :
100 g. gruyère per person / 3 shallots / oil, vinegar, salt, pepper.

Cut the gruyère into thin sticks 2-3 cm long and season with a vinaigrette dressing. Leave to soak well.

Salade de gruyère is served as an hors-d'œuvre before dinner or on a saveloy salad (mixed salad). This mixed salad often precedes an Alsace sauerkraut as part of the copious meals served here.

Asperges d'Alsace
Asparagus salad

2.50 kilos asparagus / salted water.

Tie the washed and peeled asparagus into bundles weighing about 500 g. Cover and cook for 25 minutes in salted boiling water (they must remain firm). Drain on a cloth and serve on an asparagus dish separating the fragile heads. Serve with three sauces (mayonnaise, vinaigrette, mousseline) and to accompany boiled or smoked ham (served with a hollandaise or white sauce).

Asparagus was planted for the first time in Alsace in 1873 by Pastor Heyler at Hoerdt in Bas-Rhin. He had come from Philippeville in Algeria where asparagus was grown. He was struck by the difficulties of the local peasants who struggled to gain a meagre living from the soil which was infertile but readily lending itself to the cultivation of asparagus. Pastor Heyler experimented himself with the first plantings and soon had many followers. Today the small town of Hoerdt is known as the « capital of asparagus » ; a modest monument on the wall of the chapel was erected to the memory of Pastor Heyler.

Asparagus of equal excellence is grown at Horbourg in Haut-Rhin.

Tarte à l'oignon
« Zeewelkueche » or « Zeewelwaïa »
Onion Tart

250 g. pâte brisée (see p. 43) / 500 g. onions / 100 g. smoked bacon cut into small strips / 2 dl. cream / 2 dl. milk / 2 egg yolks / 50 g. flour / salt, pepper, nutmeg.

Line a flan-dish with the pâte brisée. Preheat the oven to hot. Slice onion and fry gently. Spread in a layer over the pastry. Blanch the bacon and arrange on the onions. Mix cream, milk and beaten eggs with flour, salt, pepper, nutmeg and pour over the onions and bacon. Cook in a hot oven for about 25 minutes.

Béchamel sauce may be used instead of the egg, milk and cream mix.

Tarte flambée
« Flammekueche »
Flambéed tart

500 g. bread dough / 2 large chopped onions / 4 cl. thick cream / 60 g. smoked bacon cut into strips / 1 soup spoon colza oil / salt, grated nutmeg, pepper.

Roll out the dough thinly, place on a baker's oven peel or flat oven tray : cover with onions, bacon and seasoned cream : sprinkle over with the oil. Cook in a very hot oven or if possible in an old-fashioned open bread oven heated by flames which will flambée the tart. To be eaten piping hot.

Suggestions :
1. Leave out the onion and bacon.
2. Enrich the cream-onions-bacon mixture with 100 g. cream cheese.
3. Garnish the dough with quartered potatoes and cream.

Before cooking bread the « tarte flambée » is cooked in an open oven heated by a pine log fire or vine branches. It has to be « licked » by the flames and is eaten before a good soup or accompanied by a glass of « Kirsch ». This peasant dish can also be served either as an entrée or on its own with a good Alsace wine.

Onion tart.
(Photo S.A.E.P.)

Tarte Flambée.

(Photo taken at the « A l'Aigle »
restaurant in Pfulgriesheim
by E.H. Cordier)

Quenelles de foie
« Lewerknepfle »
Liver dumplings

250 g. pork or cow's liver / 100 g. breadcrumbs / 125 g. fairly fatty smoked bacon / 100 g. onions / 50 g. fine semolina / fresh parsley / 1 clove garlic / 2 eggs / salt, pepper, nutmeg / 3 lit. salted water / a little oil.

Fry the onions with the garlic. Soak the breadcrumbs in some milk and press. Mince these ingredients with the liver and bacon. Place mixture in a bowl. Add beaten eggs, semolina and finely chopped parsley. Season and mix thoroughly. Mould the « quenelles » into egg shapes with the aid of two spoons dipped in hot water. Poach in simmering salted water (about 12 minutes).

The liver quenelles are served hot sprinkled with croûtons or fried onion rings, accompanied by a green salad. They are also served with a traditional sauerkraut.

Suggestion : The water used to poach the quenelles makes excellent broth especially with the addition of chopped parsley, fine vermicelli or small grilled or oven-cooked croûtons.

A popular national dish in Alsace, « quenelles de foie » appear in the oldest volumes of Germanic gastronomy. The King of Bavaria, Maximillian (of the Two Bridges) was particularly fond of them, so much so that he brought a « maker of veal/liver quenelles » to court in Munich. She was « Madame Kayser », an Alsace lady, the widow of an army surgeon who had been under the Prince's command.

Fondue aux ognions et aux œufs
« Kachelmues »
Onion and egg fondue

1 kg. peeled onions / 1 table spoon flour / 100 g. butter / 1 pot fresh cream / 1-2 eggs per person / 1 glass milk / salt, ground cayenne pepper.

Chop onions and fry in butter until transparent. Season with salt and pepper (5 dessert spoons onions required per person). Add 1 table spoon of flour to the pan, moisten with a few spoonfuls cold milk (avoid curdling). Cook on a low heat ; add 2 spoonfuls fresh cream and mix well. Proceed until all the cream has been mixed in. To this fairly thick sauce add the thickly sliced hard boiled eggs. Serve with jacket potatoes which have been kept warm in a towel in an earthenware dish.

This recipe from the Vale of Villé dates back to the Middle Ages. The « Kachelmues » are served after potato soup and are followed by goat's cheese and a glass of « William's pear » liqueur.

Escargots à l'alsacienne
« Schnecke »
Snails à l'alsacienne

4 doz. fresh snails / 1 lit. stock (1/2 water, 1/2 white wine, bouquet garni, carrot, onion, shallot, thyme, bay leaf) / salt, pepper / 250 g. butter / finely chopped parsley, shallots, garlic / an escargot dish.

Clean the snails by sprinkling with coarse salt, flour and vinegar and leave for about two hours. Rinse well and blanch for 5 minutes. Rinse again and remove from shells. Discard the black parts of the snails and wash the shells.

Stew the snails gently in the stock detailed above (2 hours). Remove the snails and reduce the stock by boiling for a few minutes. Serve the snails with the stock poured over.

Preparation of butter for the snails :

Finely chop the parsley, shallots and garlic and mix with the butter, salt and pepper incorporating all the ingredients well. Into each shell place a little cooking stock, a little of this butter, and a snail before filling the rest of the shell with the butter.

Place the prepared snails on a snail-dish (making sure that the butter does not run over during cooking) and cook in a hot oven for about 10 minutes. Serve in their shells when the butter begins to foam.

It would appear that the Romans used snails in their cooking and knew how to improve their flavour. In Alsace it was the monks who introduced them to the menu at Lent ! The monasteries and châteaux had their snaileries where snails were bred and encouraged to reproduce. The monks would then sell the snails to local connoisseurs. The snaileries of the Capuchins of Colmar and Weinbach were particularly famous.

Fried carp. (Photo A. Loviton)

Escargots à l'alsacienne. (Photo S.A.E.

Truites au bleu. (Photo S.A.E.)

Carpe frite du Sundgau
Sundgau fried carp

1 fine live carp / 3 eggs / 125 g. flour / salt, pepper / a little lemon juice.

Kill the carp at the last moment, scale and wash. Cut into steaks about 3 cm thick. Wipe each steak well and dip into the seasoned beaten eggs, and then in the flour. Fry in very hot oil until brown. Remove the fish a second time in the hot oil. Serve the carp steaks well browned with boiled potatoes and slices of lemon.

Truite au bleu, au beurre fondu
Poached trout with melted butter

2 litres court-bouillon / 1 trout per person / 2 table dessert warm vinegar for each trout / 200 g. butter / parsley / salt, pepper / 3 lemons.

Obtain live trout and stun just before preparation. Clean with caution, rinsing the insides of the trout without rubbing with fingers. Pour 2 dessert spoons warm vinegar over each trout and plunge into the boiling court-bouillon. Poach gently for 5-8 minutes depending on size. Meanwhile, melt the butter and add a little salt, pepper and a few dashes of lemon juice. Serve the trout in the court-bouillon or on a plate surrounded by lemon wedges and parsley. Before tasting sprinkle over a little melted butter and some lemon juice.

The « au bleu » method of cooking is reserved principally for freshwater fish and demands special preparation in that the fish should be live and handled as little as possible before being cooked rapidly without rinsing inside too severely. This method dates back to the Middle Ages ; in those far-off days gourmets would ask for fish cooked in beer or wine.

Tranches farcies et roulées
« Fleischschnacka »
Stuffed meat rolls

Noodle pasta dough / leftover cooked meat / 1 onion / 1 clove garlic / parsley / salt, pepper / 50 g. butter / 1 glass oil.

Roll out the noodle pasta dough (see recipe) into a sheet 3 mm thick. Finely chop the leftover meat, onion, garlic and parsley. Adjust the seasoning and mix thoroughly. Spread the mixture over the pasta and roll up like a « Swiss roll », sealing the edges with warm water. Cut the stuffed pasta roll into sections (about 5 cm long), dust with flour and fry in the butter and oil until brown on all sides. Then add 1/2 litre of hot stock to the pan and allow to simmer on a gentle heat for 20 minutes. Serve with green salad.

This dish is prepared in Haut-Rhin, in miners' households in Wittenheim for example. It is an excellent, economical dish.

Tourte de la vallée de Munster
« Türt »
Vale of Munster pork pie

1 kg. minced shoulder pork / 2 eggs / 1 bread roll soaked in cream or milk / 2 medium onions / 75 g. butter / 2 cloves garlic / salt, pepper, nutmeg, a pinch of clove powder / chopped parsley / 750 g. flaky pastry.

Soak the bread roll overnight and mash with a fork. Slice the onions and brown in the butter. Mix with the pork, egg, bread roll, chopped parsley, crushed garlic, a pinch of clove powder and the grated nutmeg. Season and mix thoroughly.

Line a pie-dish (« Türteplat ») with a layer of the flaky pastry allowing it to fall over the sides. Place the meat filling in the shape of a dome on the pastry and draw up the sides over it. Cover with a pastry lid but do not prick. Brush with egg to glaze and use the tip of a fork to produce a country-style decorative effect.

Bake in a fairly hot oven for about an hour.

This pie may be eaten for main course meals accompanied by green salad.

Even in the XIth century the Alsacian Pope Leo IX showed his appreciation of « tourte ». It is a very ancient, popular speciality, the recipe being handed down from mother to daughter. It is usually prepared at the beginning of winter at the same time as the « charcuterie ». It is eaten during social gatherings and often appears in wedding receptions.

Stuffed meat rolls. (Photo A. Loviton)

Vale of Munster pork pie. (Photo E.H. Cordier)

Boulettes de viande à la sauce blanche
« Fleischknepfle » or « Fleischklösse »
Meatballs in white sauce

250 g. veal and bones / 250 g. quite fatty pork / 50 g. butter / 2 medium-sized onions / 2 eggs / fresh parsley / salt, pepper / 1 clove, nutmeg / sprig thyme / 2 table spoons flour.

Soak the breadcrumbs and drain. Chop one onion and fry gently in a little butter until transparent. Mince the meat and add the eggs, breadcrumbs, onion, parsley, thyme and flour. Season with salt, pepper and a little grated nutmeg. Knead the mixture well and leave to rest for 15 mins. Make stock from the veal bones, bouquet garni, onion, clove, salt and pepper. Shape the mixture into little balls (about 50 g. each) and poach them in the stock for about 10 minutes.

Make a white sauce with a roux base (50 g. flour). Add the remaining stock from the meatballs, season and pour this sauce over the meatballs. Sprinkle with fresh parsley.

Alternative : The veal may be replaced by beef. A small quantity of fresh cream or some capers may be added to the white sauce. The white sauce may be replaced by a hot horse-radish sauce.

The meatballs may be served with pasta, rice or patatoes. They are often made in the Wissembourg region during the « open door » or « welcome to the village » festivities.

Potée aux navets salés
« Süri Ruewe »
Salted turnip stew

1.5 kg. turnips grated on a sauerkraut shredder and pickled in brine / 500 g. smoked pork shoulder (schiefala) / 1 large onion / 2 cloves garlic / 1 large glass Alsace white wine (Sylvaner) / 200 g. smoked bacon / 150 g. lard or 1 glass oil / salt, pepper.

Slice the onion and brown in oil or fat. Rinse the salted turnips in several changes of water, drain and press. Place the onions in a casserole dish and cover with a layer of turnips. Then add the meat bacon and garlic. Spread the remainder of the turnips over the top and add the wine and a glass of water or stock. Cover the casserole and simmer gently for about 2 hours.

A few grated carrots may be added to this tasty winter peasant's dish.

This method of preserving carrots was mentioned as long ago as the Middle Ages.

Palette de porc fumée au raifort
« Schiefala »
Smoked pork shoulder with horse-radish

1 smoked pork shoulder about 1.2 kg. in weight / court-bouillon with 4 carrots, 1 medium-sized onion, 1 sprig parsley, 1 small leek.

Hot horse-radish sauce :
200 g. finely grated horse-radish / 1 small tub fresh cream / 30 g. butter / a little good stock / salt, small teaspoon sugar / nutmeg.

Simmer the pork shoulder in the court-bouillon for 1 1/2 hours (in the absence of a court-bouillon simmer from cold in plain water). Drain and cut into slices. Serve hot surrounded by potato salad or plain boiled potatoes, small pickled onions and gherkins. Prepare the hot horse-radish sauce as follows and serve in a sauce-boat :
- Make a roux with the butter and flour. Slowly add the stock and the finely grated horse-radish. Mix well and stir in a further small amount of stock if necessary and a pinch of salt (the horseradish should swell slightly). Allow to cook on gentle heat for about 15 minutes. Thicken with fresh cream. Add the grated nutmeg and serve the sauce hot with the shoulder of pork.

If the sauce is not sharp enough add a drop of wine vinegar.

« Schiefala » is a recipe typical of the Haut-Rhin and is served with a green salad or cooked in a good sauerkraut.

Pommes de terre aux oignons et au lard
« Roïgabrageldi »
Potatoes with onions and bacon

1.500 kg. potatoes / 200 g. smoked bacon / 3 large onions / 200 g. butter / salt / cast-iron casserole dish.

Line the bottom of the casserole with thin rashers of bacon. Cover with a layer of sliced potatoes and then a layer of sliced onions. Season. Continue alternating layers of potatoes and onions and knobs of butter. Finish with a layer of potatoes dotted with butter. Cover the casserole and cook for I hour in a very hot oven. Before serving mix thoroughly all the ingredients.

« Roïgabrageldi » is preferably served with smoked neck of pork and green salad.

This unique dish was eaten in the small farmhouses of the Vale of Munster and was cooked slowly in a pot buried in the cinders of the fire. « Roïgabrageldi » was also the main course for the woodcutters and charcoal burners in our forests. Nowadays it may be found in all the holiday farmhouses in the Vosges mountains.

Smoked pork shoulder with horseradish. (Photo S.A.E.P.)

Potatoes with onion and bacon...

... served. (Photos E.H. Cordier)

Potée boulangère
« Baeckeoffe »
Baker's stew

500 g. leg of beef / 500 g. boned pork loin / 1 pig's tail and 1 pig's trotter (optional) / 500 g. boned mutton shoulder / 250 g. onions / 2 cloves garlic / 2 leeks, white parts only / 1/2 litre dry white Alsace wine (Riesling or Sylvaner) / 1 bouquet garni, parsley / 1 sprig thyme, salt, pepper, 3 bay leaves, a little powdered cloves / 1.5 kg. potatoes / earthenware cooking pot plus lid.

Cut up the meat and marinade for 24 hours in the white wine, spices, some sliced onions, the bouquet garni, the white parts of the leeks and the pepper. The following day peel and slice the potatoes, place in the bottom of the cooking pot, cover with a layer of the remaining sliced onions, then the meat. Complete with a layer of potatoes and onions. Strain the marinade into the casserole and add the white wine and a little water. The liquid should half-fill the pot. Add the vegetables and the marinade spices and season. Place the lid on the pot and seal with a paste made from flour and water. Cook in a baker's oven for about 3 hours (therm. 5-6).

Serve this stew in the pot accompanied by a green salad.

Suggestions :
  - Add a few sliced carrots to the marinade.
  - « Baeckeoffe » may also be made with only two sorts of meat (beef and pork).
  - Add a few slices of goose to the « Baeckeoffe » meat.

In days gone by, housewives in Alsace, on washdays or when busy in the fields, would take this stew to the baker and let it cook in his oven after the bread was done. This dish must simmer for a long time in slow, regular heat and makes a really hearty meal on a cold winter's day.

Choucroute à l'alsacienne
« Sürkrüt »
Sauerkraut à l'alsacienne

1.5 kg. white sauerkraut / 100 g. goose fat / 2 medium-sized onions / 1 bay leaf / 1 good glass Alsace wine (preferably Riesling) / 1/4 lit. stock / 1 clove garlic / 10 juniper berries / salt, pepper / 4-5 coriander seeds.

Garnish :
1 smoked pork shoulder / 6 Strasbourg sausages / 10 liver quenelles (see recipe) / 400 g. smoked bacon / 1 small hock / 250 g. grilled white sausage / if desired, 750 g. salted pork loin / 6 medium-sized potatoes.

Wash the sauerkraut in cold water once or twice depending on the time of the year. Drain and press to extract all the water. Slice the onions and fry gently in the goose fat (in the absence of goose fat use lard or oil). Add the sauerkraut and then a small muslin bag containing the garlic, cloves, bay leaf, juniper berries and coriander seeds. Add the white wine and stock (water may be used instead of stock) and season lightly. Cover the casserole and allow to cook gently for an hour. After a good hour's cooking stir the sauerkraut, add the salted pork loin and the smoked bacon and simmer for 1 1/2 hours being careful to ensure that it does not boil dry. Then place the peeled potatoes on top of the sauerkraut where they will cook in the steam (about 1/2 hour). Meanwhile simmer the pork shoulder fairly rapidly in boiling water (1 hour 30 minutes). 20 minutes before serving poach the hock, the liver quenelles and the Strasbourg sausages and grill the white sausage. Pile the sauerkraut onto a hot dish and garnish with slices of pork loin, smoked pork shoulder, bacon, Strasbourg sausages and grilled sausages. Serve surrounded by the liver quenelles and the potatoes and crown with the hock. This « royal sauerkraut » should be eaten very hot accompanied by a good Alsace white wine or a very cold beer !

Traditionally each housewife has her own method of cooking sauerkraut. It is a unique dish which must be followed by a very light dessert. Towards the end of winter it becomes necessary to wash the sauerkraut well as it begins to « ferment » and becomes bitter.

Choucroute à l'alsacienne.

(Photo taken at the Winstub « Au Meiselocker » in Strasbourg by E.H. Cordier)

Baker's stew.
(Photo A. Loviton)

Coq au riesling
Chicken in white wine

1 chicken weighing 1.5 kg. / 4 shallots / 75 g. butter / 100 g. cream / 1 egg yolk / 15 cl. Riesling white wine / 1 small cup stock / 1 clove garlic / fresh parsley / 1 table spoon flour / 1 liqueur glass cognac / 150 g. mushrooms / salt, pepper, a little nutmeg / 2 table spoons oil.

Singe the chicken and quarter. In a casserole brown the chicken pieces in half the oil and butter for 5 minutes over gentle heat. Season and add the finely chopped shallots, parsley and garlic frying until brown. Pour over the cognac and flambé. Add the Riesling and the stock. Simmer gently for 30 minutes. Slice mushrooms, fry in rest of butter and add to the casserole. A few minutes before serving mix the flour, cream and egg yolk and add to the chicken pieces taking care not to allow it to boil. Adjust the seasoning and serve very hot with noodles or « spaetzle à l'alsacienne ».

Coq à la bière
Chicken in beer

1 chicken weighing 1.5 kg. / 33 cl. pale ale / 4 shallots / 100 g. butter / 1 large tub cream / 200 g. mushrooms / fresh parsley / salt, pepper / 1 small glass gin or Alsace « marc » brandy.

Singe and quarter the chicken. Clean and slice the mushrooms. Fry the chicken pieces in 50 g. butter and a little oil. Add the finely chopped shallots and the mushrooms. When they are well browned pour over the spirits and the beer. Season and simmer on a gentle heat for about 1 hour or until the chicken is tender. Shortly before serving arrange the chicken pieces in a deep dish and keep hot. On a high heat reduce the sauce by half, add the cream to thicken and the rest of the butter. Whip the sauce until it foams and pour over the chicken. Sprinkle with finely chopped fresh parsley and serve hot accompanied by noodles « à l'alsacienne ».

Oie farcie de la St-Martin
« Martinsgans » or « Wyhnachtsgans »
St. Martin stuffed goose

1 goose weighing approx. 6 kg. / 500 g. minced pork / 1 egg / parsley / 4 shallots / 1 small sprig thyme / 200 g. breadcrumbs / salt, pepper, nutmeg / goose liver.

Singe, clean and truss the goose. Mix and knead the different ingredients of the stuffing. Chop the goose liver and add. Stuff the goose with this mixture and sew up. Brown the goose all over in goose fat over a high heat. Then place the goose in a medium oven and roast in its own juices (about 1/2 hour per kg. for a young bird).

The stuffed goose is served surrounded by chestnut purée or whole chestnuts cooked in a little stock firstly and then in the juices from the roasting pan.

In many families stuffed roast goose still constitutes the « plat de résistance » on Saint-Martin's Day (11th November) the festivities often continuing for 2 days and nights. Once considered a sacred animal the plump goose has now become a symbol of prosperity. At Christmastime, a celebration which reconciles Earth to Heaven the menu is determined by the three elements : « earth », « water » and « air ». Hence the preference of the ladies of Alsace households for hare, carp and goose.

Civet de lièvre
« Hasepfeffer »
Jugged hare

1 hare or 1 rabbit weighing approx. 2.5 kg. / 2 large onions / 3 cloves garlic / 1 bouquet garni / 2 glasses oil / 1 small glass cognac / thyme, bay leaf, cloves, salt, pepper / 50 g. butter / 50 g. flour / 100 g. bacon cut into strips / 1/2 lit. red wine / 200 g. mushrooms / nutmeg.

Cut the hare into pieces and retain the blood and liver discarding the intestines. Marinade for 24 hours in the wine, a glass of oil, the cognac, sliced onions, crushed garlic, and spices and stir from time to time. Next day, brown the bacon in a little butter and the remainder of the oil. Dry the pieces of hare thoroughly, add to the pan and brown. Then add the marinade spices. Sprinkle with flour and cook until it turns brown. Add the marinade juices and the bouquet garni and cook on a gentle heat (1 hour 30 minutes). Fry liver in a little butter and oil in another pan.

A little before the end of the cooking time thicken the sauce with the hare's blood. Slice the onions, fry and add to the hare. Simmer for a few minutes. Remove the pieces of hare and place in a warmed serving dish. Strain the sauce over them. Serve piping hot accompanied by noodles « à l'alsacienne ».

Jugged rabbit. (Photo A. Loviton)

Chicken in riesling. (Photo S.A.E.P.)

Choux rouges aux pommes et aux marrons
« Rotkrüt mit Aepfel un Keschte »
Red cabbage with apples and chestnuts

1 large red cabbage / 125 g. goose fat or 1 large glass oil / 2 large pippin apples / 1 bay leaf / 2 cloves / 1 glass wine vinegar / salt, pepper, a pinch of sugar / 20 to 25 peeled chestnuts or a tin of unsweetened chestnuts.

Wash, remove central stalk from cabbage and shred the leaves. Marinade for about 30 minutes in a large dish with the vinegar, salt, pepper and sugar. Slice the onion and fry in the fat, cover with the cabbage, add the cloves, bay leaf and vinegar and, finally, a little stock. Cover and allow to cook gently for about 2 hours. Peel the apples and chestnuts and add 30 minutes before the end of cooking time being careful not to mix the ingredients. Before serving piping hot, remove the spices, adjust the seasoning and pile the cabbage onto the serving dish with the chestnuts on top. Serve as an accompaniment to roast pork, goose, duck or beef.

Suggestion. Fry onions and bacon in the fat, add the cabbage and season. Pour over a little vinegar and stock. Cook for 2 hours and serve with sliced smoked sausage and mashed potatoes.

Galettes de pommes de terre
« Grumbeerekiechle » or « Grumbeeredatscherle »
Potato cakes

1 kg. potatoes / 1 large onion / chopped parsley / 2 eggs / 1 table spoon flour / 1 glass oil / salt, pepper, nutmeg.

Wash and peel the potatoes and onion. Grate coarsely, drain and retain the potato starch which runs off. Mix the starch with the grated potatoes and onion, the eggs and the chopped parsley. Season and mix all the ingredients well. Using a table spoon make potato cakes out of the mixture. Slide into hot oil in a frying-pan, press down with a spoon browning on both sides.

The cakes are served crisp accompanied by a green or cucumber salad or unsweetened apple jelly. It usually follows a soup course and is part of the menu for a day without meat or forms a country evening meal.

Nouilles à l'alsacienne
« Selbschtgemachti Nüdle »
Noodles à l'alsacienne

300 g. flour / 200 g. fine semolina / 6 eggs / 1 glass water / 1 dessert spoon salt.

Place the flour and semolina in a pile on a noodle board and make a well in the centre. Dissolve the salt in the water and pour into the well together with the eggs. Knead the dough well and shape into balls the size of an egg. Cover with a cloth and allow to rest for about 1 hour.

Roll out each « egg » individually, dust lightly with flour, and cut into strips (about 3-4 mm wide). Arrange these pasta ribbons on a cloth.

When the noodles are completely dry they may be preserved in a tin. When ready for use boil them in plenty of salted water for about 20 minutes.

It is thought that noodles first appeared in Alsace after the 30 Years war according to a recipe which probably came from Italy. They were already mentioned in a collection of recipes by a monk in Lucelle Abbey in 1671 under their present name.

Spätzle à l'alsacienne
« Wasserschtriwle » or « Mehlknepfle »

300 g. flour / 3 eggs / a little water / 1 tea spoon salt / 4 lit. salted water / 50 g. butter / fried croûtons.

Mix the flour, eggs, water and salt with a wooden spatula until a « runny », not too thick, dough is obtained. Roll out the dough and, using the edge of a board and a knife dipped in salted boiling water, cut into thin strips. Boil in a large pan for long enough to allow them to come to the surface. Then rinse in cold water, drain and sauté in a little butter. Before serving garnish with croûtons fried in butter.

They are marvellous accompaniments for a good sauerkraut or jugged hare.

Potato cakes. *(Photo E.H. Cordier)*

The preparation of noodles. *(Photo E.H. Cordie*

Gnocchis à l'alsacienne
« Grumbeereknepfle » or « Buewespietzle »

1 kg. raw potatoes / 500 g. jacket baked potatoes / 150 g. flour / fine salt / 1 large tub fresh cream / 2 large onions / 75 g. butter / boiling salted water.

Wash, peel and grate fairly coarsely the raw potatoes. Press in fine cloth to extract the juice and the starch (leave to rest for 15 minutes). Peel the baked potatoes and pass through a vegetable mill. Mix the grated raw potatoes, the mashed cooked potatoes, the starch (not the juice) the flour and the salt. Knead the mixture well. Chop the onions and fry gently in the butter until brown. Dust hands with flour and shape the dough into « quenelles » about 10 cm long. Poach in the boiling salted water (8 minutes). Drain and cover the gnocchis with a mixture of onions and warm cream. Serve as accompaniments to roast pork or veal with a green salad.

Quenelles de pommes de terre cuites
« Schneeballe » or « Grumbeereknepfle »
Potato dumplings

1.5 kg. jacket baked potatoes / 250 g. flour / 3 eggs / a little chopped parsley / 75 g. bread croûtons fried in butter / fine salt / salted boiling water / 1 tub fresh cream.

Peel and mash the baked potatoes, add the salt, eggs, chopped parsley, flour, and half the fried croûtons. Carefully mix all the ingredients and shape into balls the size of an egg. Poach in salted boiling water for 5 minutes (the quenelles should rise to the surface). Drain and arrange in a deep dish and cover with the rest of the croûtons and the warmed cream. Serve with green salad, or with braised red cabbage or as an accompaniment to roast pork.

Gnocchis au fromage
« Kaesknepfle »
Cheese gnocchis

300 g. flour / 300 g. cream cheese / 2-3 eggs / table salt / 80 g.
butter / salted boiling water.

Mix the flour and the cream cheese in a mixing bowl. Add the eggs
and salt (and then a little pepper). Leave to rest for 10 minutes. Using
two soup spoons dipped in boiling water shape the dough into balls
the size of an egg. Poach for 10 minutes. Drain and serve these cheese
gnocchis with hot melted butter poured over them.

Cheese gnocchis were mentioned as long ago as Antiquity (called
« globi » by the Romans who ate them during the 3rd Punic war). In
Alsace this very ancient dish is still called « Kaesspaetzle ». In the
Baden area they are still called « Kaesspatzen ».

Gnocchis de semoule ou croquettes de semoule
« Griesknepfle » or « Griesschniette »
Semolina gnocchis or semolina croquettes

1 lit. milk / 200 g. semolina / 100 g. butter / 1 small teaspoon
salt / grated nutmeg / 2 egg yolks.

Boil the milk with half the butter and salt. Add the semolina a little
at a time stirring until the mixture thickens. Remove from the heat
and add the egg yolks and nutmeg. Spread this mixture on a large
board or a tart plate, leave to cool for 1 hour, then using a knife or
pastry cutter, cut into diamond or rectangular shapes. Fry until
golden in the remainder of the butter. These gnocchis are served after
soup accompanied by a green salad or apple sauce for a really
nourishing supper.

Gnocchis de semoule (alternative recipe)
« Griespflutte »
Semolina gnocchis

Same ingredients as for semolina croquettes. One may, if desired,
leave out the eggs and add a good pinch of salt.

Prepare the batter in the manner described for semolina
croquettes, Drop table spoonfuls of this batter into a buttered gratin
dish, firstly coating the spoon with melted butter. Shape the gnocchis
into ovals and cover with melted butter and bake in a hot oven. Serve
accompanied by apple sauce, stewed prunes or dried pears.

Farmhouse cream cheese. (Photo A. Loviton)

Cream cheese with cream and kirsch. (Photo E.H. Cordier)

Fromage blanc à la paysanne
« Bibbeleskäs »
Farm house cream cheese

500 g. farm cream cheese / 1 medium tub fresh cream / salt, ground pepper / herbs (parsley, chives) / 1 finely chopped clove garlic / 1 finely chopped large onion.

Beat the cream cheese with the cream in a mixing bowl and season lightly. Serve fresh with jacket baked potatoes or spread on home-made bread. According to individual taste add freshly ground pepper, chives or chopped parsley, garlic and chopped onions, either together or separately. Season lightly. In the absence of chives use very thin slices of leek.

In some houses in the country it is eaten for supper unsalted accompanied by damson jam or dried fruit preserve, home-made bread or even jacket potatoes !

Fromage blanc au kirsch et à la crème fraîche
« Siaskas »
Cream cheese with kirsch and fresh cream

Add a little rennet to 1 lit. fresh warm milk. Leave until it coagulates (1 hour). Cut the curdled milk up into slices and leave to sweat (45 minutes). Before serving place in a pine mould, remove and cut the day-old cream cheese up into small portions. Serve covered with fresh cream and sprinkled with sugar and kirsch.

This very nourishing dish is eaten in the Vale of Munster and all the farmhouses offering accommodation in the Vosges mountains.

Le fromage de Munster
Munster cheese

Authentic Munster cheese is eaten either raw or sprinkled with cumin accompanied by home-made bread or jacket baked potatoes and butter.

It is usual to take with it a glass of Gewurztraminer or Pinot noir, or even a tankard of beer. These are the traditional « regional accompanying drinks » but do not exclude it being served with a full-bodied « Munster », a good red wine.

The origin of Munster cheese probably dates back to the XIIth century when Irish monks settled in the Vale of Saint-Grégoire and experimented with the production of cheese in their monasteries (« Munster » comes from the word « monastery »).

Pâte levée
Leaven pastry

250 g. flour / pinch salt / 2 egg whites / 10 g. yeast / 60 g. butter / 1 small glass warm milk / 40 g. sugar (for sweet dishes).

Place 50 g. of the flour in a mixing-bowl, make a well in its centre, add the yeast and mix in a little of the warm milk. Fold in the flour so as to form a large soft ball of dough (the leaven). Cover with a cloth, leave in a warm place until it doubles in size.

Place the rest of the flour in a mixing bowl, make a well in its centre and pour in the warm milk, melted butter, salt and sugar. Mix all these ingredients, add the egg whites and the leaven dough. Knead well until it forms bubbles when raised and comes away cleanly from the sides of the bowl.

Leave until it doubles in size.

Pâte brisée
Short crust pastry

200 g. flour / 100 g. butter / 1 pinch salt / 1 small glass water.

Place the flour on a pastry board and add the salt. Dip fingers in flour and rub the butter in until the mixture ressembles fine breadcrumbs.

Make a well in its centre and add the water, mixing gradually with the fingertips until a soft pastry dough is obtained. Knead 2 or 3 times with the palms of the hands.

Leave to rest for 1/2 hour before using.

For fruit tarts add 30 g. caster sugar.

A whole egg may be added thus reducing the amount of water required slightly.

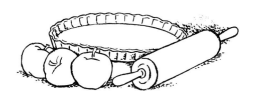

Cheesecake.
(Photo E.H. Cordier)

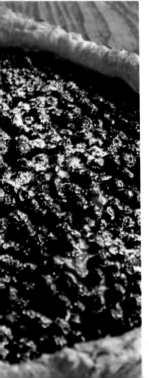

Bilberry tart.
(Photo A. Loviton)

Tarte au fromage blanc
« Kaeskueche »
Cheesecake

300 g. pâte brisée (see recipe) / 300 g. cream cheese / 4 eggs / 125 g. sugar / 2.5 cl. milk / small tub cream / 50 g. potato starch / 25 g. flour / vanilla-flavoured sugar / a little grated lemon peel.

Line a tart dish with the pastry. In a bowl mix the cream cheese with the 4 egg yolks and the sugar. Add the potato starch and mix in slowly the milk, cream, vanilla and grated lemon peel. Beat the egg whites until stiff and fold gently into the mixture. Fill the pastry case with this mixture and bake in a hot oven for 30 minutes.

After cooking turn the tart out of the baking dish and leave upside down on a grill until it cools to prevent the cheese sinking and to obtain a smooth surface. While still warm turn the tart upright and dust with icing sugar. Serve.

Suggestions : raisins may be added to the cream cheese or it may be sprinkled with ground roasted almonds.
- The tart case may be filled with a mixture of confectioner's custard and cream cheese. Add egg whites beaten stiff (the tart case must be cooked beforehand for 20 minutes covered with dried vegetables). This variation was usually made on Sundays or feast days.

Tarte aux « Riwele »
« Riwelekueche »
Riwele tart

1 large plateful peeled, cored and sliced apples / 100 g. butter / 150 g. sugar / 350 g. flour / 1 egg / 1 packet vanilla-flavoured sugar / 1 spoonful « kirsch » (brandy) / 1/2 packet baking powder.

Mix the butter, sugar, egg, vanilla-flavoured sugar, flour and baking powder in a bowl. Knead well and roll the dough out between the fingers to form thin « quenelles » (riwele). Place 3/4 of the « riwele » on a buttered oven dish, add the sliced apples and lay the remainder of the « quenelles » on top. Cook in a medium oven for 30 minutes. Leave to cool before serving.

Tarte aux quetsches
« Quetschelkueche » or « Zwatschgawaïa »
Damson tart

250 g. pâte levée or pâte brisée (see recipes) / 1 kg. damsons / 100 g. sugar / powdered cinnamon / icing sugar.

Butter a deep pie-dish and line with pastry. Stone and quarter the damsons then arrange in concentric circles on the pastry. Dust with 100 g. sugar and powdered cinnamon and cook in a hot oven for 30-40 minutes. Turn out onto a grill and dust again with sugar and cinnamon. Damson tart may be eaten warm or cold.

Tarte aux pommes
« Apfelkueche » or « Aepfelkuacha »
Apple tart

250 g. pâte brisée / 1 kg. apples / 2 eggs / 1 tub cream / 1 cup milk / 125 g. sugar / powdered cinnamon / 1 sachet vanilla-flavoured sugar.

Line a buttered tart dish with the pastry. Peel the apples and quarter or cut into eighths if they are large (make slits in the sides of these to facilitate cooking). Arrange in concentric circles on the pastry. Dust with sugar and cinnamon. Bake in a very hot oven for 25 minutes. When the apples are baked cover with a mixture of eggs, milk, cream, sugar and vanilla. Bake for approx. 20 minutes more. After cooking turn the tart out onto a grill and dust with icing sugar and cinnamon. The tart may be served warm or cold.

Suggestion : all sorts of fruit may be used - pears, cherries, mirabelle plums, bilberries. The orchards of Alsace and the Vosges forests are laden with good quality fruit. Very often an evening meal will consist of vegetable soup followed by a tasty fruit tart.

Tarte aux myrtilles
« Heidelbeerekueche »
Bilberry tart

250 g. pâte brisée / 1 kg. bilberries / 2 spoons sugar.

Line a pie-dish with the pastry.
Fill with fruit. Bake in the oven and dust with sugar when cooked.

Damson tart. *(Photo A. Thiébaut/S.A.E.P.)*

Apple tart. (Photo E.H. Cordier)

Tranches à la cannelle ou Pain perdu
« Armi Ritter » or « Zimtschnitte »
Cinnamon slices or bread cakes

6 slices stale bread / 1/2 lit. warm milk / 2 eggs / sugar to taste / powdered cinnamon / 50 g. butter / 100 g. breadcrumbs.

Soak the bread slices on both sides in the milk and then the beaten eggs. Coat with breadcrumbs and then fry on both sides in the butter. When golden brown place on a warm plate and dust with sugar and ground cinnamon. They are served warm and should be eaten when still soft. They may also be served with apple sauce or any other stewed fruit.

Suggestion : soak the slices of bread in red wine then in pancake batter. Then proceed as directed.

Petites cuisses de dames
« Schenkele »
Little ladies' legs

350 g. flour / 200 g. caster sugar / 4 eggs / 100 g. butter / 125 g. powdered almonds / 1 dessert spoon kirsch / 1 pinch table salt / flavour to individual taste from : cinnamon, grated lemon peel, orange-blossom water.

Mix the sugar and eggs until a fairly thick constituency. Add the flour, melted butter, almonds, salt, kirsch.

Knead well and leave the dough to rest for about 2 hours.

Cut the dough up into strips about 10 cm long and roll on a board into little sausages about the thickness of a finger. Brown in quite warm, but not hot, oil. Dust with icing sugar.

Pâte à frire
Batter mix

125 g. flour / 2 eggs / 1 pinch salt / 1 spoonful sugar / 1 large glass pale ale.

Place the flour in a basin, make a well in its centre and add all the ingredients except the whites of the eggs which should be placed to one side. Using a large wooden spoon mix all the ingredients together gradually to form a soft dough. Leave to rest for at least one hour.

When ready for use beat the egg whites until stiff and fold in gently.

This batter is intended for use in preparing fruit fritters : apples, cherries, damsons.

Beignets aux pommes
Apple fritters

Core the apples, peel and cut into slices about 1/2 cm thick. Dip in the batter and fry in hot oil.

Remove from the pan when they rise to the surface golden brown. Dust with sugar.

Beignets de Carnaval
« Fasenachtskiechle »
Shrovetide doughnuts

500 g. flour / 1/4 lit. warm milk / 3 dessert spoons sugar / 2 eggs / 1 table spoon kirsch / 75 g. butter / 1 pinch salt / 20 g. brewer's yeast.

Sift the flour into a bowl, make a well in the centre and add all the ingredients. Mix well until a soft, light dough is obtained. Roll out into a sheet about 1 cm thick, and then cut into squares, diamonds and circles (with a glass). Fry until brown in medium hot oil. Drain then dust with sugar and cinnamon or icing sugar.

These doughnuts may be eaten alone or with a fruit preserve.

In the past, they were given to the children, the priest and the teacher of the village, in memory of the souls of the dead (a custom dating back to Mediaeval days). Even today children and conscripts go from house to house collecting « beignets » during the Shrovetide bonfires or firework display (« Schieweschlawe »). In the country, apparently the first « beignet » out of the fat was given to the hens, an infallible way, it was said of making them good layers.

Steamed bread rolls.
(Photo E.H. Cordier)

Shrovetide doughnuts.
(Photo E.H. Cordier)

Petits pains gonflés à la vapeur
« Dampfnüdle » or « Hefepfannekueche »
Steamed bread rolls

500 g. flour / 1/4 lit. warm milk / 60 g. butter / 2 eggs / 30 g. baker's yeast / a little oil / salt / large dessert spoon sugar.

Gradually stir the sugar, salt and yeast into the warm milk and add the butter. Place in a bowl and add the flour and the eggs. Knead the dough well and leave to rise for one hour. Roll out into a sheet about 3 cm thick then cut into a circular shape with a glass or a cutter. Leave to rise for a further 30 minutes. Heat the oil and a little butter in a cast-iron pan with a lid. Place the pieces of leaven dough well apart in the pan then immediately add 3/4 glass of water. Cover the pan at once and cook until a golden crust appears on the rolls. These « Dampfnudles » make a complete evening meal and are eaten with dried fruit preserve, tinned fruit salad or cream with white wine.

Suggestion : place the pieces of dough in a well-buttered dish : pour some milk into the bottom (about 1 cm deep). Cover and cook in the oven for 35 minutes. A little before serving, uncover and add a small tub of thin cream and a dessert spoon of sugar. Cover again and cook in the oven until all the cream has been absorbed ; the « Dampfnüdle » will be slightly caramelised.

Crème au vin blanc
« Wyncrem » or « Wynsoss »
Cream with white wine

3 eggs / 3 dessert spoons sugar / 2 dessert spoons potato starch / 1 1/2 glasses good Alsace wine / 1/2 glass water / a little grated lemon peel.

Beat the three egg yolks with the sugar until light and fluffy ; add the flour then the white wine, water and grated lemon peel. Whisk over a very low heat taking care not to boil. Remove from heat and beat for a further minute, cool the cream by placing the bowl in cold water. Stir until cold. Whisk the egg whites and fold in gently. Serve in individual bowls decorated with small macaroons.

Mendiant or clafoutis
« Bettelmann »
Beggarman

6 stale rolls or the equivalent quantity of bread / 4 eggs / 40 cl. warm milk / vanilla-flavoured sugar / 125 g. sugar / powdered cinnamon / 2 dessert spoons « Kirsch » / 50 g. raisins soaked in the « Kirsch » / 50 g. butter / 750 g. apples or cherries.

Grate the crust of the rolls or the stale bread and mix the crumbs with nutmeg. Boil the milk with the vanilla-flavoured sugar and pour the boiling liquid on the rolls or bread to soak them. Mash with fork or by hand. Then add the egg yolks, sugar, raisins, « Kirsch », the thinly sliced apple or whole cherries. Beat the egg whites until they are stiff then gently fold into mixture. Pour into a buttered tin, dust with the mixture of crumbs and cinnamon and dot with butter. Cook in a hot oven for 1 hour.

The cake may be eaten hot, warm or cold, after a good vegetable soup and can be kept for several days.

Chinois
« Schneckekueche » ou « Rosekueche »
Chinaman

500 g. flour / 125 g. butter / 5 g. salt / 80 g. sugar / 1/4 lit. warm milk / 1 egg white / 20 g. yeast / powdered cinnamon / 100 g. ground almonds / 100 g. raisins / a little icing sugar / 1 small glass Kirsch.

Make the pastry as for Pâte levée (p. 43).

Roll out into a sheet 4 cm thick and cut into 6 strips (depending on the size of cake tin). Brush the surface with a little melted butter, sprinkle with sugar, ground almonds, cinnamon and raisins.

Roll up the strips of pastry and arrange on the dish with one « snail » in the middle. Leave for 1/2 hour. Glaze with egg and cook in a medium-hot oven for 45 minutes. After cooking cover with icing sugar soaked in Kirsch.

Chinaman.
(Photo E.H. Cordier)

Beggarman.
(Photo E.H. Cordier)

Kugelhopf or Gugelhupf cake

500 g. flour / 200 g. butter / 100 g. sugar / 2 eggs / 1/4 lit. milk / 1 tsp. salt / 50 g. seedless raisins / approx. 50 g. almonds / 25 g. baker's yeast.

Warm milk gently. Retain 1/2 glass, slowly stir in the yeast and leave to expand. Add the butter, sugar and salt to the remainder. Place the flour in a bowl, make a well in its centre, crack in the eggs and add the above mixture. Mix well, knead and turn the dough occasionally to allow it to absorb as much air as possible (in the old days it would be kneaded for 1/2 hour). When the dough no longer sticks to the board add the yeast and continue to knead the dough (« klopfe ») for a few moments. Then place back in the bowl and cover with a cloth. The dough should be left to rise in a warm place (approx. 1 hour). When the dough is well-risen add the raisins soaked in warm water. Butter the Kugelhopf dish and sprinkle the almonds in each of the sections. Lay the dough carefully in the dish and leave to rise until it reaches just above the top of the cake-mould. Bake in a medium oven for about 45 minutes. The Kugelhopf should be golden brown in colour. The cake may be protected by foil placed on top during cooking. Serve dusted with icing sugar for Sunday breakfast or as a dessert accompanied by a glass of good Alsace wine (Gewurztraminer or Riesling).

This cake probably originated in Austria and became fashionable at the time of Marie-Antoinette. Its round shape recalls the XIVth headresses called « Gugelhuete » (cf. « Gogel »).

Gâteau aux « Streusel »
« Streuselkueche » or « Straïselkueche »
Streusel cake

Pâte levée :
300 g. flour / 1 egg / 100 g. butter / 25 g. sugar / 15 g. baker's yeast / 1 glass milk.

Mix the yeast in a little warm milk and allow to expand. Mix all the ingredients together, knead then add the yeast. Knead again to obtain a consistent texture breaking the dough several times. Roll out into a sheet approx. 3 cm thick and use it to line a pie-dish. Brush surface with beaten egg and cover with a layer of « Streusel » prepared as follows.

Streusel :
100 g. sugar / 100 g. butter / 100 g. flour / 1 tsp. powdered cinnamon.

Melt the butter, add the flour and mix the two ingredients together. Mix the sugar and the cinnamon, and knead well. Chill then crumble this mixture in an irregular layer on the pâte levée. Leave the cake dough to rest and rise for 1 hour. Bake in a medium oven for 30 minutes. Dust with icing sugar before serving.

Pain de fruits secs
« Bierewecke » or « Hutzelbrod »
Fruit loaf

250 g. dried pears / 125 g. dried figs / 125 g. dried, stoned prunes / 100 g. raisins / 100 g. dates / 50 g. candied orange peel and lemon peel / 50 g. chopped almonds / 50 g. hazel nuts / 100 g. walnuts / grated rind of 1 small lemon / cinnamon / 200 g. bread dough / a little grated nutmeg / 1 tsp. ground star anise / 1 glass « kirsch » / 1 pinch powdered cloves / 50 g. sugar.

Soften the dried pears by cooking in water and, in the juice obtained, stew the prunes gently. Then cut the cooked fruit into thin strips together with the figs, dates, orange and lemon peel. Chop the almonds, the hazel nuts, and the walnuts (retain a few for decoration) and mix with the finely sliced fruit. Add the grated lemon rind, cinnamon, grated nutmeg, powdered clove and ground anise. Pour over the kirsch and the juice from the cooked fruit and leave to soak overnight covered with a clean cloth. The following day add 50 g. of sugar and mix all the ingredients well with the crumbled bread dough. Knead the mixture well so as to bind the fruit together. Then shape the dough into a long oval loaf, brush with egg-yolk to glaze and cook in a moderate oven (1 hour).

These fruit loaves keep for several days and are made at Christmas time. In terms of Christian symbolism the nuts and almonds represent the divine message. Inside the hard shells lies the hidden fruit which can only be eaten when the outer skin is broken. « Bierewecke » was served before midnight mass with ginger bread and a hot drink.

Crêpes à l'alsacienne
« Eierkueche »
Alsace pancakes

300 g. flour / 1/4 lit. milk / salt / 6-8 eggs depending on size / 50 g. butter / oil.

Place the flour in a mixing-bowl and add the beaten eggs to the well in its centre with the salt and the milk. Beat the mixture well. Heat the oil and butter in a heavy frying-pan and cover the bottom with a thin layer of the batter. Cook on a low heat, toss the pancake and brown on other side. Serve immediately with sugar, a fruit preserve, or creamed cheese. These pancakes may also be accompagnied by a green salad and make an excellent supper dish.

« Streusel » cake. (Photo E.H. Cordier)

Fruit loaf and Christmas cake. (Photo E.H. Cordier)

Gâteau de Noël
« Chrischtstolle »
Christmas cake

500 g. flour / 250 g. butter / 1/8 lit. warm milk / 3 large dessert spoons sugar / 1 packet vanilla-flavoured sugar / 1 egg / 50 g. candied orange peel / 50 g. candied lemon peel / grated rind of 1 lemon / 200 g. chopped almonds (including some bitter almonds) / 125 g. currants / 125 g. sultanas / 1/2 tea spoon fine table salt / 40 g. baker's yeast / 1 dessert spoon rum or brandy / 1 pinch cinnamon.

Place the flour in a warmed mixing-bowl and make a well in its centre. Add the egg, warm milk, sugar, melted butter, vanilla-flavoured sugar, cinnamon, grated lemon rind, salt and yeast. Mix well and add the chopped walnuts, lemon peel and orange peel, as well as the dried fruit soaked in brandy or rum. Knead well to obtain a firm but supple, light dough, and add a little warm milk if necessary. Cover with a cloth and allow to rise for 2 hours in a warm place or near to a stove. On a floured noodle-board make a long cob with the dough. Roll it out into a thick layer and fold one half over the other. Brush the dough with water. « Chrischtstolle » should be presented in this unique manner resembling a cloth folded in two. Allow to rise a second time, brush with melted butter and bake in a hot oven until golden brown. Remove from oven, brush again with melted butter and sprinkle with icing sugar.

This cake can also be baked in a cake-tin.

The strange shape of the « Chrischtstolle » recalls the swaddling-clothes of a new-born babe. In the past, the cake was not cut until 28th December in memory of the massacre of the innocents by King Herod in Jerusalem.

Petits fours de Noël au beurre
« Butterbredle »
Christmas petits fours with butter

Mix the sugar, eggs, softened butter, and flour. Knead well and allow to rest for approx. 2 hours. Roll into a sheet about 4 mm thick and cut up into a variety of shapes using a pastry-cutter. Brush with egg yolk to glaze and bake on a buttered baking-tray in a moderate oven for about 10 minutes.

Petits fours de Noël aux amandes
« Schwowebredle »
Christmas petits fours with almonds

500 g. flour / 250 g. butter / 250 g. sugar / 250 g. almonds or ground hazel nuts / 100 g. candied orange peel / grated rind of 1/2 lemon / 2 eggs / 1 egg yolk for glazing / 1 pinch baking powder / 10 g. powdered cinnamon.

Mix the softened butter with the sugar, eggs, ground almonds, or hazel nuts, candied orange peel, grated lemon rind, cinnamon, salt and baking powder. Knead well and fold in the flour. Add a third egg yolk if necessary. Leave the dough to rest overnight in a cool place. Roll out the dough on a board without dusting with flour (3-4 mm thick) and cut into a variety of shapes with a pastry cutter (hearts, stars, birds, trefoils, people, dogs, etc.). Brush the little cakes with egg yolk to glaze and bake in a moderate oven on a buttered tray (10 minutes).

Petits fours à l'anis
« Anisbredle »
Petits fours with aniseed

600 g. flour / 500 g. sugar / 6 medium eggs / 2 dessert spoons aniseed.

Beat the eggs and sugar for 20 minutes until stiff. Add the aniseed, fold the sieved flour in carefully (obtaining a firm dough). Using two small spoons place small amounts of the dough on a buttered, lightly floured baking-tray (the dough should not run). Bake the next day in a moderate oven. The tops of the petits fours should rise and remain white on a small golden base.

Petits fours à l'Ancienne
« Springerle »
Old fashioned petits fours

4 eggs / 500 g. sugar / 500 g. flour / grated peel of 4 lemons / aniseed.

Mix the egg whites and sugar then the yolks and the peel. Beat for 30 minutes and add 500 g. flour. Leave for 1 hour. Roll into a sheet 1 cm thick and press on the floured block of motifs.

Cut designs out with a knife, place on a baking tray sprinkled with aniseed, and leave overnight.

Cook until the base is golden brown.

Kugelhopf. (Photo E.H. Cordier)

Old-fashioned petits fours. (Photo E.H. Cordier)